HOW TO MAKE BASIC HOSPITAL EQUIPMENT

Designs by: S. W. Eaves & A. Platt
J. Procter
I. M. Stewart
K. J. McCubbin & D. C. Simpson
J. Mee & D. Scott
M. Davies
P. Bolliger

Compiled and introduced by Roger England

Published by Intermediate Technology Publications Ltd,
9 King Street, London WC2E 8HN, U.K.

ISBN 0 903031 60 4

Printed in England by The Russell Press Ltd, Nottingham.

ACKNOWLEDGEMENT

This book has been published with the assistance of the Bernard van Leer Foundation as a tribute to the work of Will Eaves. The Intermediate Technology Development Group gratefully acknowledges their assistance.

FOREWORD

Will Eaves died in a car accident on 22nd March, 1978 while travelling between Jos and Kano.

Born in 1926, Will Eaves was a skilled instrument technician. After serving in the Royal Pioneer Corps and with British European Airways as an Aircraft Instrumentation Technician, he joined the staff of University College Hospital, London in 1952 and developed the particular skills in the medical field which he later used so effectively in Nigeria. In 1957 he went to the University College Hospital in Ibadan to set up workshops for the design and manufacture of medical instruments. In 1967 he moved to Ahmadu Bello University where he carried out similar work for four more years.

In 1970 his career again took a new direction. He joined the Intermediate Technology Development Group as a Field Officer. He spent four years setting up Intermediate Technology Workshops in Zaria and Maidugari. It was during this period that many of the designs and prototypes were produced which established Will Eaves' reputation for creativity and inventiveness in turning the theory of intermediate technology into real and immediately usable practice. Arising from this came the publication *Intermediate Techniques,* still widely demanded throughout the developing world.

In 1974 he joined the Integrated Education for Development project supported by the Bernard van Leer Foundation in Jos and established training workshops for the development of relevant technology. To this he brought both his engineering skills and sensitivity to the needs of ordinary Nigerians. These workshops have concentrated on local production of articles to improve the quality of village life, creating employment opportunities for primary school leavers and contributing to the general development of rural communities.

The enduring significance of his work lies not so much in what the workshops produced as in the training methods he applied. He departed radically from the bookish approach to technical education. Trainees have become directly involved in productive work — both as individuals and as members of a group. They are thus helped to become self-reliant and aware of the importance of service to the community. They have become skilled in relevant technology not by being instructed, but by discovering how to make and do things for themselves. The Relevant Technology Workshops are a dramatic success and have been received as such by the Nigerian authorities.

Since his tragic death the Nigerian States in which he worked have shown themselves more than sensitive to the importance of his achievement. Currently, Relevant Technology Workshops and training centres are operating in Plateau, Benue and Kano States, in all five units. Perhaps more important, graduates of the workshops have slowly but increasingly shown willingness to return to their areas of origin, establishing their own training and production workshops, and building up the stock of skills which Nigeria's rural areas so badly need. It is this commitment which is in many ways the real tribute to Will Eaves' work which is illustrated in this manual.

PREFACE

There are parts of the world where the amount of money available for health services is pitifully small. A dollar a head a year buys very little when it has to cover not only salaries, drugs, etc., but also the building and equipping of health care facilities. Prices in the catalogues of even second-hand equipment are enough to deter anyone who wants to start a health centre or small hospital from scratch in one of the many underserved areas where the needs are greatest and money is scarcest.

A lot of medical equipment works just as well without the fancy finish that medical services in the industrialised countries accept as normal. It all depends on its purpose. If something can be made by local people, using simple tools and on-the-spot materials, which will do the same job as an expensive, imported item, then it should be used. The money stays in the community, more work is available, and it is always easier to maintain what has been made locally — and perhaps even to improve it with more experience. Self-reliance breeds ideas and confidence.

Of course it is true that certain medical needs can only be met by sophisticated manufacturers, but the cost of most furnishings and of simple but necessary equipment can be minimised if its function is looked at with an unprejudiced eye. In Africa, Will Eaves designed beds, trolleys, wheelchairs and other equipment made from wood, metal tubing and wheels taken from scrap heaps. These items have been made in local workshops and have proved their worth over a number of years. Similar items are being made in India and in many other countries where commonsense is more plentiful than cash. There are other related ideas being developed like the sand bed and the baby incubator included in this book. More and more will come into circulation as the concept of appropriate technology spreads and is accepted as something which is not makeshift but the best way to solve problems according to local circumstances. Each situation will be different, and every item should provide an opportunity for local entrepreneurs to use their ingenuity. Some suggestions for possible improvements to the Eaves designs are printed along with the originals.

The Intermediate Technology Development Group and the Appropriate Health Resources and Technologies Action Group are interested in knowing about other ideas such as these so that the details can be disseminated. The World Health Organisation now has a programme for Appropriate Technology for Health, which is concerned with equipment, tools and techniques likely to be of use in primary health care throughout the world. Knowledge, experience, special expertise and appropriate solutions are valuable resources which must be shared if the world's burden of disease and handicap is to be lessened. Everyone with ideas can contribute to improving the health of the community in some way, however small. The best answer to a problem can often be the simplest and even the obvious one which may, nevertheless, have been overlooked.

This book provides some simple designs which could help to provide solutions to the problems of equipping rural hospitals using local skills and local resources and materials in ways which could reduce costs considerably and still provide adequate equipment.

Katherine Elliott
Honorary Director
AHRTAG.

CONTENTS

LIST OF PHOTOGRAPHS

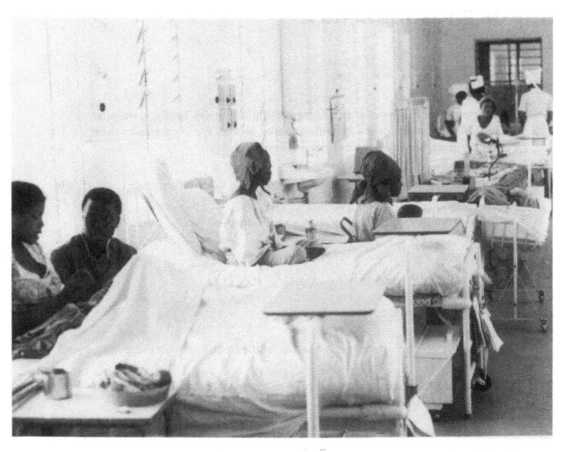

A women's medical ward at the Ahmadu Bello University Teaching Hospital, Zaria, Nigeria, refurbished with bedside tables, lockers and ward screens made by the hospital's Instrument Engineering Department.

INTRODUCTION

Why local manufacture?

A great deal of the basic but important equipment upon which health services in developing countries depend can be made locally without sophisticated or capital-intensive techniques. Not only *can* this be done but there are several good reasons why it *should* be done:-

- the equipment will be more appropriate since it is designed specifically for local needs and conditions and with the involvement of the users;
- it is easier to maintain what has been locally made and to improve it subsequently;
- it is cheaper than equipment bought from overseas manufacturers usually found in richer countries with high production and transportation costs;
- it requires little or no foreign currency and the money involved stays in the community concerned;
- it creates local employment in areas where there are invariably job shortages;
- it creates local skills and experience which can be utilised in other fields and passed on through earn-and-learn apprenticeships to poorer social groups;
- it creates self-reliance and confidence and this, after all, is what development is about.

Whilst basic locally-produced equipment can be as good or better than that which is imported, there is often opposition to its use. This sometimes comes from doctors and other medical workers especially those who have been trained abroad in hospitals with 'high finish' products. They often feel that locally-produced equipment is inferior because it does not have this veneer. Frequently they are also under some pressure from the agents of foreign manufacturers and encouraged to order imported equipment in this way. These people must be encouraged to see that locally-produced equipment can be used to greater advantage and that much of the 'high finish' on imported products is unnecessary for its efficient functioning. At the same time, however, the reasons for this opposition have to be recognised, and local manufacture should aim to achieve a reasonable appearance for equipment if this will improve its acceptability.

What equipment is needed?

There can be no list of essential equipment applicable for all places. Each situation requires its own solutions to meet its own priority needs while taking into consideration the available materials and techniques.

9

The designs and suggestions in this book are therefore illustrations. Most of the ideas were developed by the late Will Eaves at the Intermediate Technology Workshops in Nigeria and tested in use over a number of years. This simply-designed equipment — for example, beds, trolleys and wheelchairs — fulfills the basic needs for patient care in hospitals and health centres. The designs are intended to be suggestions and to be used as a guide for further developments. They do not pretend to be optimum solutions and certainly do not constitute a complete list of needs or possibilities. It is hoped that the construction ideas will have application in the manufacture of other pieces of equipment.

An area which this book does not deal with but which offers tremendous potential for local manufacture is that of laboratory equipment. Straightforward and tested designs are needed for distilled water production, for centrifuges, for effective sterilisation of syringes and other equipment, and perhaps for the manufacture of the simple glass and plastic ware used in great quantities in laboratories and in patient care. A number of useful manuals and basic laboratory equipment lists are now available and it is hoped subsequently to produce a book of designs suitable for local manufacture.

What kind of organisation is needed?

There are many ways in which the manufacture of simple hospital equipment can be organised and a range of scales on which such a venture can be established. A small unit in a district hospital may be quite adequate for producing modest quantities of equipment and will make a great contribution by servicing and repairing this equipment as well as some of the imported items. The important thing is that the equipment made is that actually needed most. Even for a small rural hospital, priorities should be established as to what equipment is to be made. It is wise to involve hospital medical staff in establishing these priorities and in the equipment design work since, in this way, they are more likely to accept the solutions and products.

If an equipment unit is to be set up at a district or regional hospital it should aim to support the primary health care services in its area. It should operate parallel to the hierarchy of services provided by the health care system since rural health centres and village community health workers also need simple equipment which is often beyond their means to make or maintain. A hospital-based equipment unit can support them in much the same way as hospital-based treatment facilities aim to support village level patient care.

The skills gained in the manufacture of health services equipment should be put to maximum use in the service of the community. In many areas, for example, health care depends on transport to take supplies to village health workers, to supervise and assist them in their work and to facilitate the referral of village patients in need of hospital care. Such transport is often unavailable because of the need for quite simple repairs which a hospital-based equipment unit could undertake. Similarly, village generators and deep-well 'donkey' engines are frequently out of action because nobody knows how to make a part for a temporary repair.

However, small hospital workshops are not really suitable for larger scale production of equipment, and for this it will be necessary to establish a manufacturing centre providing a service on a national or regional level. This will require careful planning and probably full support from the central government although there may still be scope for small private sector manufacture. Adequate studies would have to be undertaken for such larger scale production to ensure that investment is matched to the size and nature of demand. Again, each situation will demand its own approach depending on precise equipment requirements and the levels of skill available.

What help is available?

The Intermediate Technology Development Group has an Industrial Services Unit that is able to provide advice and assistance in undertaking the studies required to establish centres for the local manufacture of health services equipment.

The World Health Organisation has an Appropriate Technology for Health programme which can provide advice on a number of aspects of equipment.

The Foundation for Teaching Aids at Low Cost (TALC) is able to provide a number of useful designs, publications and visual materials.

Finally, since there is an important need to disseminate information and experiences in this field, the Intermediate Technology Development Group and the Appropriate Health Resources & Technologies Action Group endeavour to answer technical enquiries and to provide assistance. They are therefore interested in hearing about successfully-tested designs, related experiences and unfilled needs so that this information can be passed on to others with similar problems or with suitable experience to offer.

Roger England

Useful addresses

Intermediate Technology Development Group,
9 King Street,
LONDON WC2E 8HN, U.K.

World Health Organisation,
Appropriate Technology for Health Programme,
1211 GENEVA 27, SWITZERLAND.

Foundation for Teaching Aids at Low Cost,
3 Jersey Lane,
St. Albans,
HERTS AL4 5AD, U.K.

Appropriate Health Resources & Technologies Action Group Ltd.,
85 Marylebone High Street,
LONDON W1M 3DE, U.K.

BASIC TOOLS AND MATERIALS

Suggestions for basic tools:

General purpose hacksaw
Sheet metal hacksaw
Monodex sheet metal cutter
Sheet metal shears
Roundnose pliers
General purpose pliers
Pincers
Q-max sheet metal hole cutters
Electric arc-welding equipment

Metric spanners
Carpenter's brace and augers
Twist drills
Hand drill
Centre punch
Soldering iron
Light and heavy weight hammers
Pop riveting gun.

Non-essential but desirable tools:

Oxy-acetylene welding equipment
Electric drill

Pipe bender
Angle iron 'snip, notch & bend'.

Whilst these last items are desirable and indeed essential for any larger scale production, they can be dispensed with if necessary. A pipe bender could be constructed from available materials and welding can be replaced by modified designs using nuts and bolts, epoxy-resin glues and fibreglass tape.

Basic materials:

The most commonly used materials include:

¾" electrical conduit tubing
½", ¾", 1" galvanised iron (GI) tubing
1½" X 1½" X $\frac{1}{8}$" mild steel angle
Small diameter mild steel rod, e.g. $\frac{1}{8}$", ¼"
18 and 24 gauge sheet iron
Plywood
Bicycle components.

Remember that the open ends of piping and tubing should be sealed with plugs or in other ways which avoid the accumulation of dirt inside the tubing. The use of locally available materials should be maximised and there is much scope for (tested !) innovation and experiment. Although most of the equipment described in this book is constructed from the above materials, some designs of rattan and bamboo are also included (see pages 85 and 86).

DESIGNS FROM THE
INTERMEDIATE TECHNOLOGY WORKSHOPS
ZARIA, NIGERIA

FOLDING HOSPITAL BED

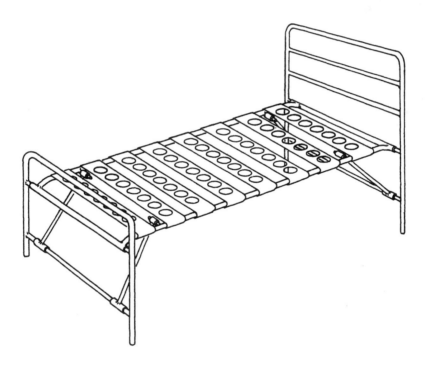

Note: Drawings and sketches are not to scale.

This bed is suitable for permanent use in hospitals or health centres but can be easily folded for stacking in storage and for easy transportation. It is constructed largely from galvanised iron and conduit tubing. This design shows the use of mild steel springs but these can be replaced by a variety of locally available materials including wood, canvas, string or matting.

A useful refinement would be to weld a 12" length of ¾" GI tubing to one of the outside vertical uprights of the bed head to function as the scabbard for a drip stand. (See the same arrangement on the hospital patient's trolley design.)

Construction

First construct the head frame — Diagram 1.

Materials: A — ¾" diameter GI tube

               B — ¾" diameter conduit tube

               or other similar-sized tubings such that one will fit inside the other.

The 35" length and the two 4" lengths of GI tube must be free to rotate on the conduit tubing.

DIAGRAM 1

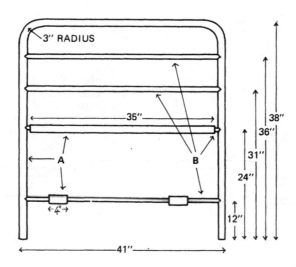

Then construct the tail frame in a similar way — Diagram 2.

DIAGRAM 2

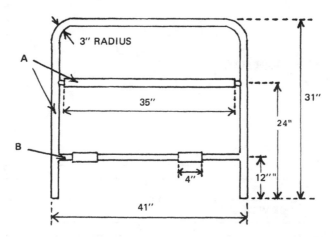

Assemble the bed frame by welding the two side support tubes to the 35" lengths of GI tube on the head and tail frames. The support tubes should be bent slightly at each end as shown to allow the bed to fold flat — Diagram 3.

Materials: Support tubes — ¾" diameter GI tube

               Tie rod locating pegs — ¾" diameter conduit tube.

15

Welding should be done whilst the bed is in a folded position and correct alignment is essential at this stage.

DIAGRAM 3

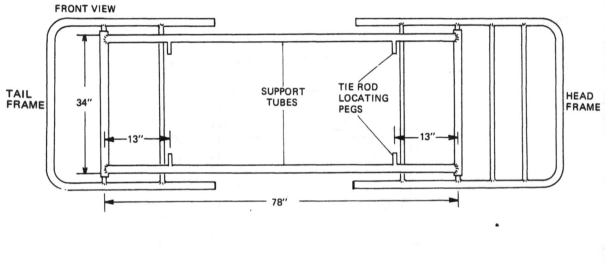

Construct the four tie rods — Diagram 4.

DIAGRAM 4

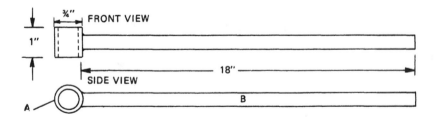

Locate the tie rods on the locating pegs and weld the tie rod ends to the 4'' GI tubes on the head and tail frames. Ensure that the frames are perfectly vertical before welding — Diagram 5.

DIAGRAM 5

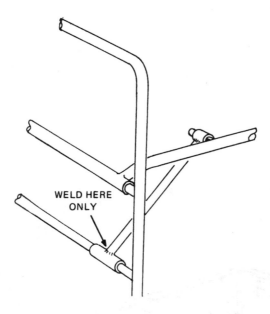

WELD HERE
ONLY

Construct the spring plates — Diagram 6 (or other means of mattress support).

Materials: 18 gauge mild steel plate, 8 pieces each 41″ × 9″.

The spring plates should have 10 holes of 2″ diameter equally spaced along the centre line. The ends of the springs are bent around the support tubes and fixed by two pop rivets at each end.

DIAGRAM 6

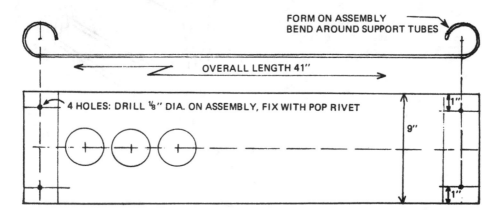

FORM ON ASSEMBLY
BEND AROUND SUPPORT TUBES

OVERALL LENGTH 41″

4 HOLES: DRILL ⅛″ DIA. ON ASSEMBLY, FIX WITH POP RIVET

1″

9″

1″

All welded areas are cleaned and the whole assembly painted.

FOLDING BED

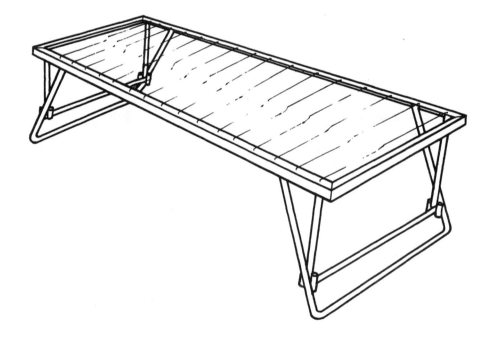

This is a more basic bed without head or tail frame. The support frame is made from mild steel angle and the legs from conduit tubing.

The bed can easily be folded for storage or transportation. The vertical leg supports fold up to lie parallel to the bed ends whilst the sloping legs fold up parallel to the bed sides.

The springs shown in this design are made from small diameter rods but these can be replaced by any suitable local material such as wood, canvas, string or matting.

Shows the way in which the legs and the vertical leg supports are folded.

Construction

First construct the bed frame — Diagram 1.

Materials: 1½″ X 1½″ X ⅛″ mild steel angle.

Mark out the dimensions on a single length of angle if possible so that there will be only one weld in the middle of one end as shown. If only shorter lengths are available use two lengths and locate the second weld in the middle of the other end.

DIAGRAM 1

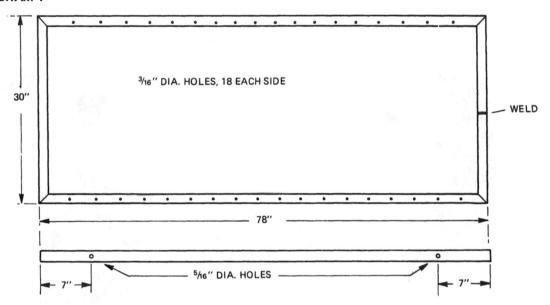

3/16″ DIA. HOLES, 18 EACH SIDE

30″

WELD

78″

5/16″ DIA. HOLES

7″   7″

The corners are formed by cutting out 90° wedges from the top face of the angle and bending them squarely until the edges of the cut come into contact with each other — Diagram 2. They can be welded together for additional strength.

DIAGRAM 2

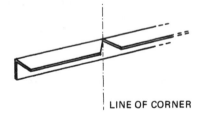

LINE OF CORNER

When the frame is completed drill 18 holes of 3/16″ diameter equally spaced down the top angle of each side support and ½″ in from the open edge of the angle. These are to attach the springs. Then drill a hole of 5/16″ diameter in the vertical angle of each side support a distance of 7″ from each end, i.e. a total of four holes. These are to attach the sloping legs.

The next step is to construct the sloping legs — Diagram 3.

Materials: ¾″ conduit tube

The open ends of the legs are heated and beaten flat so that, after rounding the edge of each flat with a file, a ¼″ hole can be drilled through.

DIAGRAM 3

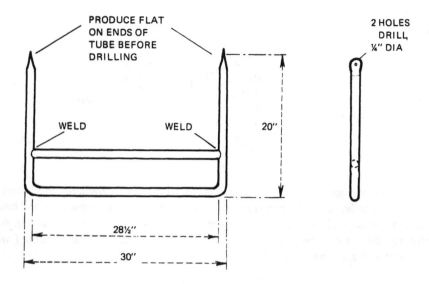

PRODUCE FLAT
ON ENDS OF
TUBE BEFORE
DRILLING

2 HOLES
DRILL,
¼" DIA

WELD   WELD

20"

28½"

30"

Next construct the four vertical leg supports — Diagram 4.

Materials: ¾" conduit tube.

DIAGRAM 4

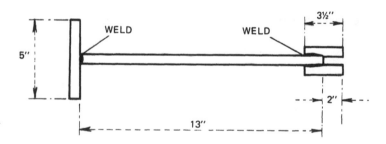

WELD   WELD

3½"

5"

2"

13"

Cut three pieces of 1" X 1" X ½" mild steel angle each 1" long to use as hinge brackets for the vertical leg supports and weld these brackets to the underside of the bed frame with the vertical leg supports in position — Diagram 5.

DIAGRAM 5

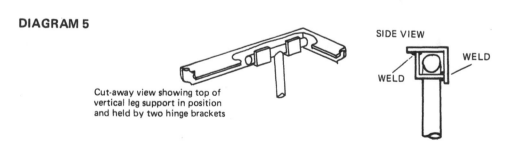

SIDE VIEW

WELD

WELD

Cut-away view showing top of
vertical leg support in position
and held by two hinge brackets

The sloping legs are next attached to the bed frame using ¼" diameter bolts and nuts — Diagram 6.

DIAGRAM 6

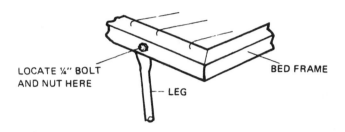

LOCATE ¼" BOLT
AND NUT HERE

LEG

BED FRAME

Construct the 18 springs each 30" long and made from $^3/_{16}$" diameter mild steel rod. Bend the ends to fit into the holes in the bed frame and, when fitted, tighten the rods and create a spring effect by making a small kink in the centre of each rod as shown in the title drawing. A simple key tool is useful for this. It can be made from a short piece of wide diameter tubing with grooves cut in one end and with a bar handle at the other — Diagram 7.

DIAGRAM 7

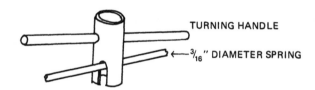

TURNING HANDLE

$^3/_{16}$" DIAMETER SPRING

Finally clean all welded parts and paint.

WARD SCREEN

A simple movable screen will have many uses in the patient care areas of hospitals and health centres. This one is made mainly from conduit tubing.

The screen panels can be made from any suitable local materials like cotton, woven matting, canvas or plastic sheeting.

Although the screen is shown with wheels (and these are very convenient if floor surfaces are adequate) they are not essential. Without them the screen can be lifted into position if two people are available.

A very basic screen could be produced by omitting the base altogether and just allowing the panels to rest on the floor. In this case the height dimension will have to be increased to achieve the same overall height.

Base of a finished ward screen with screen panels of locally made curtain material.

Construction

First construct the two centre frames — Diagram 1.

Materials: Frame A — ¾" conduit tube
Fittings B — 1" GI tube.

Bend two lengths of tubing to the shape shown with one square corner. Insert the four fittings before completing the weld at point C. Weld the two ¾" fittings in position as shown but the two 4" lengths must be free to move on the frame. Drill ⅛" diameter holes in the four locations shown.

DIAGRAM 1

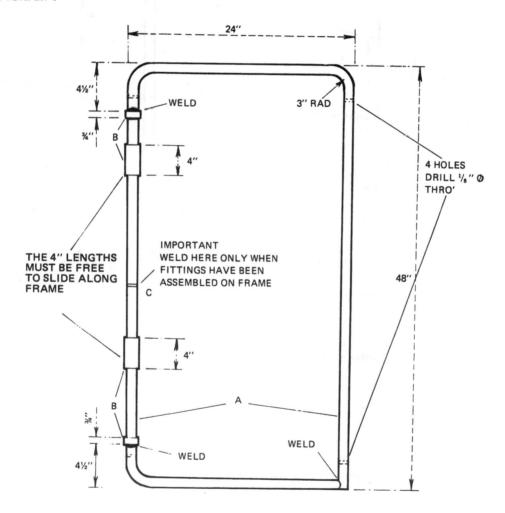

Next construct the two side frames — Diagram 2.

Materials: ¾" conduit tube.

These have no fittings but do have the four holes of ⅛" diameter as in the centre frames.

DIAGRAM 2

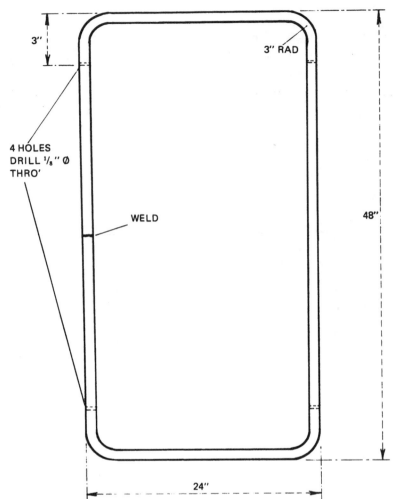

3''

3'' RAD

4 HOLES
DRILL ⅛'' Ø
THRO'

WELD

48''

24''

Construct the base frame — Diagram 3.

Materials: 1'' X 1'' mild steel section
1'' X ⅛'' mild steel strip.

DIAGRAM 3

11''

WELD

WELD

11''

22''

21''

21''

Weld the two 21″ lengths to the 22″ length to form a cross-shaped base. This joint can be strengthened by welding a 4″ length of 1″ X ⅛″ mild steel strip to the underside.

The two centre frames are next welded together — Diagram 4.

Ensure that the frames are in line before welding and weld on both sides of the join.

DIAGRAM 4

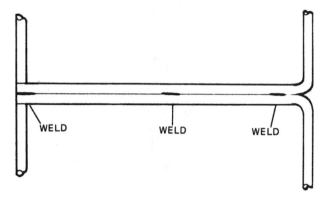

The two side frames are placed in position and each welded to the two 4″ fittings on the centre frames. The welding is done whilst the side frames are held at right angles to the centre frames — Diagram 5.

DIAGRAM 5

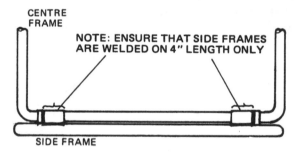

Cut two 20″ lengths of ¾″ conduit tube and weld these either side of the join of the centre frames so that 9″ of the tubes are in contact with the centre frames and 11″ protudes below. Weld the ends of these two tubes to the base frame — Diagram 6.

DIAGRAM 6

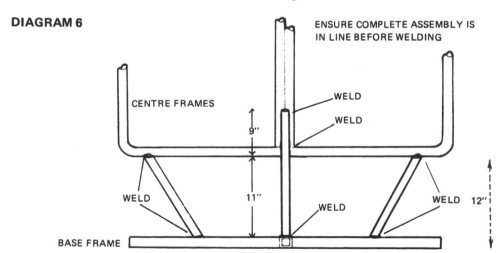

Cut two 13" lengths of ¾" conduit tube and weld these as additional supports between the centre frames and the base frames — Diagram 6.

Curtain hooks can be made from $^1/_8$" diameter wire bent around ¼" diameter rod at one end to form the hook shape, inserted in the holes in the frames and bent over and welded — Diagram 7.

DIAGRAM 7

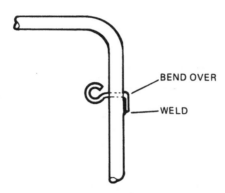

BEND OVER

WELD

Finally wheels can be attached as appropriate for the kinds of wheel available. The title diagram shows 2½" diameter industrial castors (plate fitting) welded to the base frame.

Clean all welded parts and paint. Fit expandable curtain rods between the hooks (or tie string) and attach screen material.

HOSPITAL WHEELCHAIR

This wheelchair is intended for use only in hospitals or major health centres (or for short distances outside) where floor surfaces are suitable for small wheels. The patient using this wheelchair will have to be pushed by hospital staff or by other patients or relatives.

It can be made more comfortable by the addition of a padded seat and back rest and by the provision of flat tops to the arm rests.

Planks which store behind the chair back can be used to support a patient's legs in splints.

Wheelchair designs more suitable for use outside hospital are shown in subsequent sections.

Construction

First construct the wheel frame — Diagram 1.

    Materials: ¾" conduit tube or ½" GI tube, and 1" mild steel angle.

    All joints are welded as shown.

DIAGRAM 1

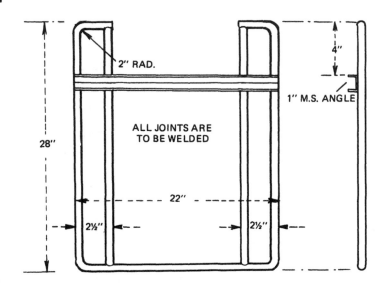

Make 4 wheel brackets for the two front wheels and weld these to the wheel frame — Diagram 2.

    Materials: 1½" X 1½" X $^1/_8$" mild steel angle.

DIAGRAM 2

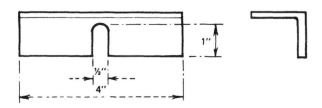

Next construct the two arm rests — Diagram 3.

Materials: ¾" conduit or ½" GI tube.

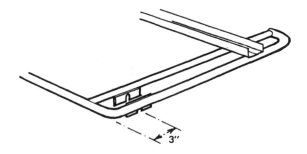

DIAGRAM 3

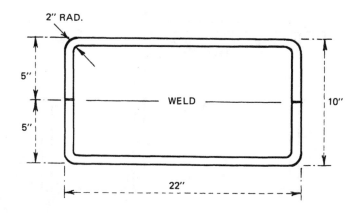

Construct the back rest — Diagram 4.

Materials: ¾″ conduit or ½″ GI tube
1″ X ⅛″ mild steel strip.

DIAGRAM 4

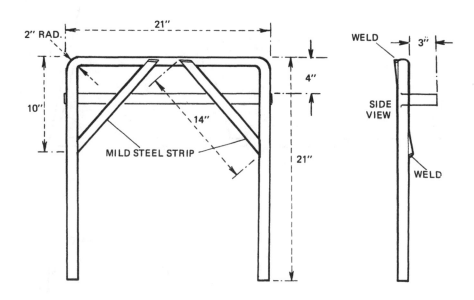

Construct the two seat supports — Diagram 5.

Materials: ¾″ conduit or ½″ GI tube.

DIAGRAM 5

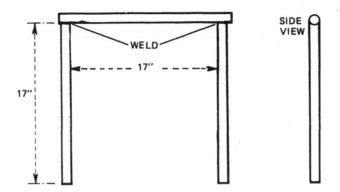

Weld the two seat supports to the wheel frame so that the distance between the tops of the two supports is 10″ and the angles are the same for each — Diagram 6.

DIAGRAM 6

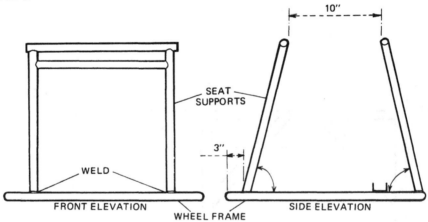

Construct the two arm rests and weld across the tops of the seat supports — Diagram 7.

DIAGRAM 7

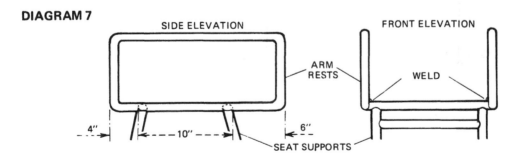

Weld the back rest to the arm rests as shown — Diagram 8.

DIAGRAM 8

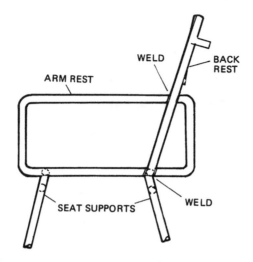

ARM REST   WELD   BACK REST

SEAT SUPPORTS   WELD

Cut out the back, seat and foot rests and drill holes to attach to the frames as shown in the title drawing — Diagram 9.

Materials: ¼" plywood.

DIAGRAM 9

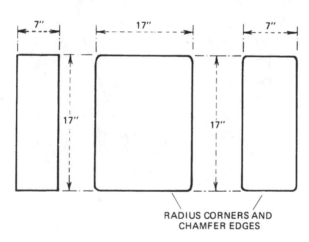

7"   17"   7"

17"   17"

RADIUS CORNERS AND CHAMFER EDGES

Attach the wheels as shown — Diagram 10.

Materials: 6" diameter X 1" wide wheels with rubber rims
2½" diameter industrial castors (swivel) with plate fittings.

DIAGRAM 10

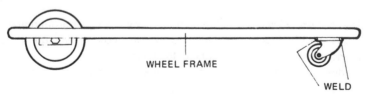

WHEEL FRAME

WELD

OUT OF HOSPITAL WHEELCHAIR

This wheelchair employs bicycle wheels to enable it to travel over rougher ground and to cushion the passenger. Again, various additions could be made to increase comfort including flat-topped arm rests, padded cushions and pannier bags for patients' belongings.

The wheelchair is shown with two handles for pushing but these could be joined by a cross bar if desired.

Finished wheelchair.

Construction

First construct the wheel frame — Diagram 1.

    Materials: ¾" conduit tube or ½" GI tube.

DIAGRAM 1

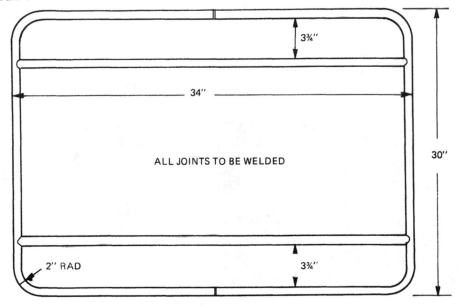

Cut off four pieces of angle for wheel brackets and cut out the sloping slots as shown — Diagram 2.

Materials: 1½" X 1½" X $^1/_8$" mild steel angle.

The slots must match so that wheels will run straight. Cutting and finishing can be done pair by pair to obtain a good match.

DIAGRAM 2

Weld brackets to wheel frame — Diagram 3.

DIAGRAM 3

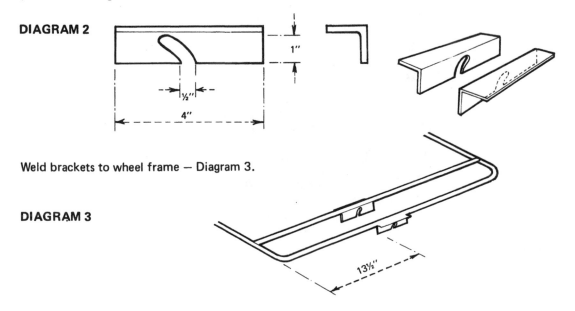

Construct the two arm rests — Diagram 4; the foot rest — Diagram 5; and the handle bar — Diagram 6.

Materials: ¾'' conduit or ½'' GI tube.

DIAGRAM 4

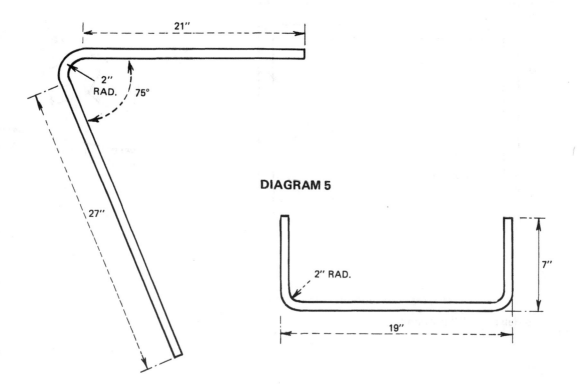

DIAGRAM 5

DIAGRAM 6

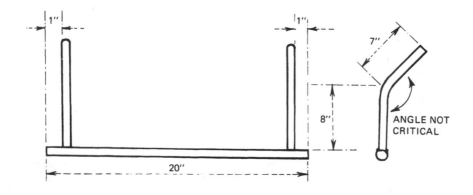

Construct the seat frame — Diagram 7.

Materials. 1½" X 1½" X ⅛" mild steel angle.

DIAGRAM 7

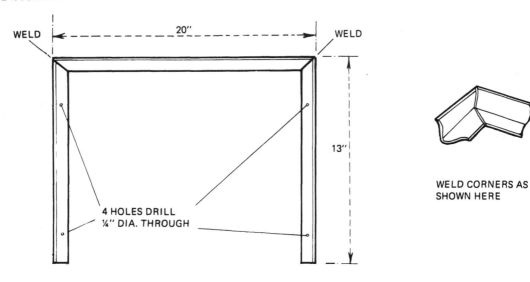

WELD

20"

WELD

13"

4 HOLES DRILL
¼" DIA. THROUGH

WELD CORNERS AS
SHOWN HERE

Cut out the back rest, seat and foot rest — Diagram 8.

Materials: ¼" plywood.

DIAGRAM 8

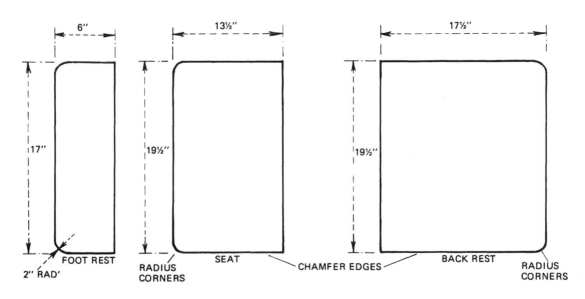

6"

13½"

17½"

17"

19½"

19½"

FOOT REST

2" RAD'

SEAT

RADIUS
CORNERS

CHAMFER EDGES

BACK REST

RADIUS
CORNERS

Fit two standard 26" bicycle wheels into the brackets and weld the arm rests and the foot rest in position on the wheel frame — Diagram 9; weld the seat frame and the handle bar to the wheel frame — Diagram 10. To obtain stability the body weight must be directly over the wheel centre. This is achieved by positioning the back of the seat above the wheel centre-line.

DIAGRAM 9   **DIAGRAM 10**

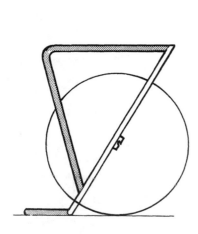   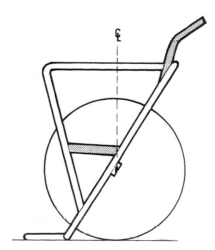

Finally weld a strip of 1½" X 1½" X $^1/_8$" mild steel angle between the tops of the arm rests and 3" from the handle bar — Diagram 11. This provides support for the back rest at approximately the right inclination.

Attach the plywood seat, backrest and foot rest. Clean all welded areas and paint.

DIAGRAM 11

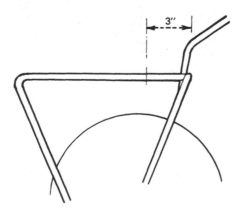

INVALID CARRIAGE WITH CHAIN DRIVE AND BRAKE

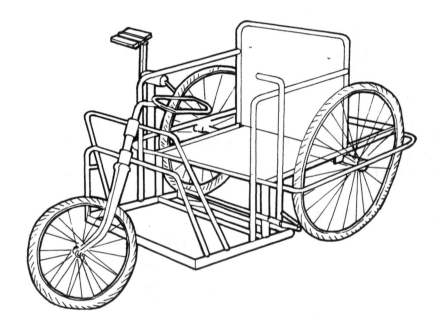

This carriage employs a number of bicycle parts and its large wheels make it suitable for a variety of road surfaces. It is self-propelled by a chain drive from a hand pedal to the right rear wheel (although this could, of course, be constructed for a left hand drive).

The carriage provides excellent mobility potential for the permanently disabled and could be fitted with a tray and storage panniers to enable its owner to earn a living in a variety of street-selling activities.

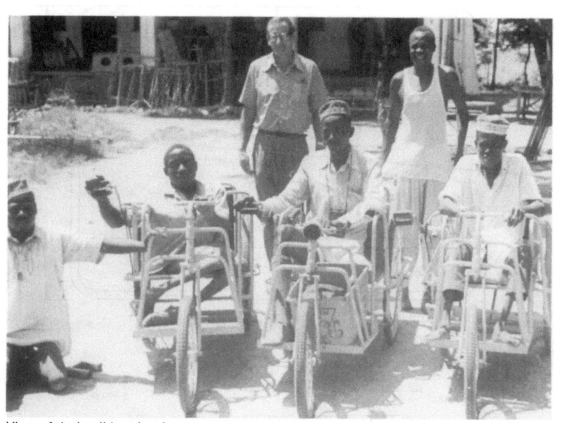

Views of the invalid carriage in use

Construction

Construct the wheel frame — Diagram 1; the back rest frame — Diagram 2; the two arm rests — Diagram 3 and the front fork frame — Diagram 4.

Materials: ¾" conduit tube
                   1" X ¹/₈" mild steel strip (for back rest supports).

DIAGRAM 1

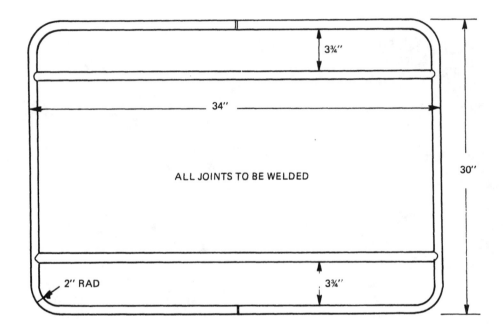

3¾"

34"

ALL JOINTS TO BE WELDED

30"

2" RAD

3¾"

DIAGRAM 2

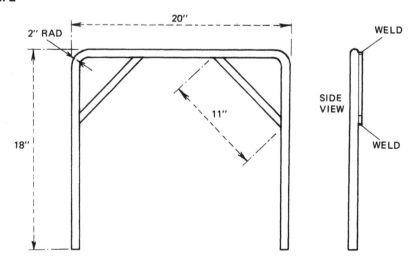

20"

2" RAD

WELD

18"

11"

SIDE VIEW

WELD

DIAGRAM 3

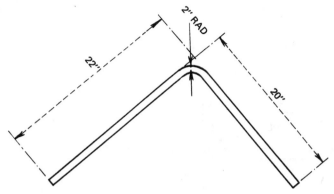

DIAGRAM 4

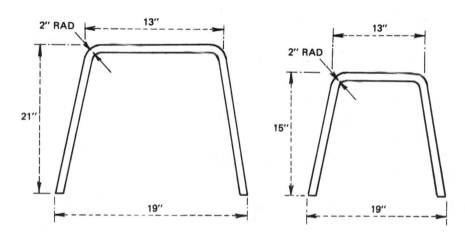

Cut off four pieces of angle and cut slots as shown for the wheel brackets and weld these to the wheel frame — Diagram 5.

DIAGRAM 5

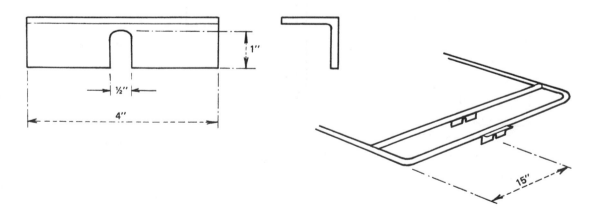

Construct the foot rest frame — Diagram 6.

Materials: 1" GI tube
1½" X 1½" X ⅛" mild steel angle.

DIAGRAM 6

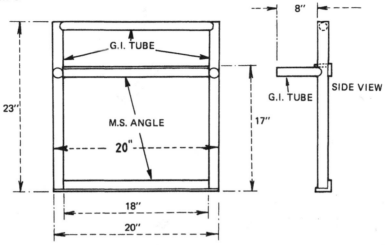

Construct the brake assembly — Diagram 7.

Materials: ¾" conduit tube
1" GI tube.

The two 4" lengths of GI tube must be free to move over the conduit and should be assembled before the frame is welded.

DIAGRAM 7

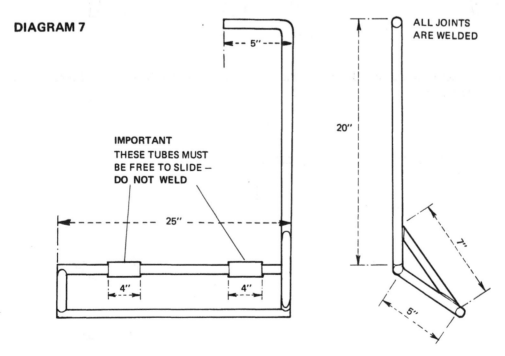

Construct the steering handle — Diagram 8.

Materials: ¾" conduit tube.

DIAGRAM 8

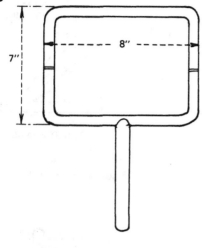

ALL JOINTS
ARE WELDED

Construct the steering column — Diagram 9.

Materials: 1½" GI tube
               1¼" GI tube.

DIAGRAM 9

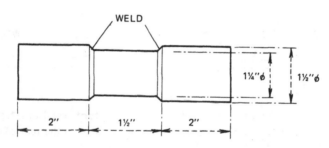

Cut out the seat, back and foot rests — Diagram 10.

Materials: ½" plywood.

DIAGRAM 10

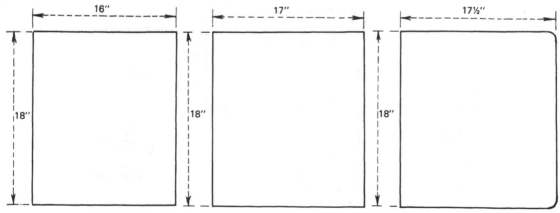

Weld the brake assembly to the uprights on the foot rest frame as shown (welding only on the 4" tubes) — Diagram 11.

DIAGRAM 11

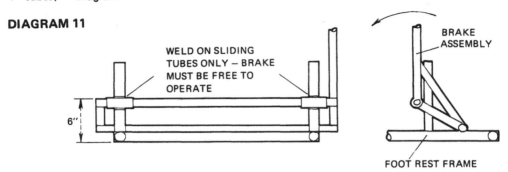

WELD ON SLIDING TUBES ONLY — BRAKE MUST BE FREE TO OPERATE

6"

BRAKE ASSEMBLY

FOOT REST FRAME

Weld the front fork frame and the steering column to the foot rest frame angled as shown so that the forks will clear the front of the foot rest frame. This angle should be judged during construction — Diagram 12.

DIAGRAM 12

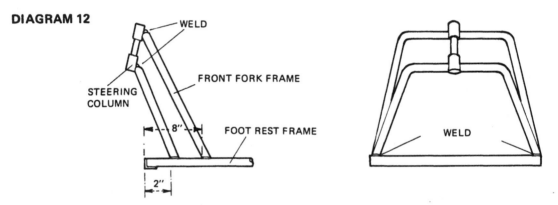

WELD

STEERING COLUMN

FRONT FORK FRAME

8"

FOOT REST FRAME

2"

WELD

Join the foot rest frame to the wheel frame by welding the foot rest frame uprights to the front edge of the wheel frame (at A) and weld two ¾" conduit struts from the rear of the foot rest frame to the rear of the wheel frame (B) — Diagram 13.

Weld the arm rests and the back rest as shown — Diagram 13.

DIAGRAM 13

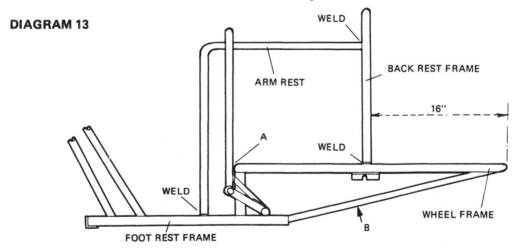

WELD

ARM REST

BACK REST FRAME

16"

A

WELD

WELD

WHEEL FRAME

B

FOOT REST FRAME

Locate the front forks into the steering column ensuring that they turn freely. Locate the steering handle through the column and the front forks and weld in position. Attach the front wheel.

Materials: Bicycle front forks
18'' diameter bicycle wheel.

Assemble the rear wheels and drive mechanism — Diagram 14.

Materials: Two 26'' diameter bicycle wheels
Two 3'' diameter gear cogs
Bicycle pedal
Bicycle pedal bearing
Bicycle chain (approximately 48'').

Locate one 3'' gear onto the outside of one wheel and weld. Locate the two wheels in their brackets.

Weld the other 3'' gear onto the bicycle pedal; push the pedal onto the shaft in the pedal bearing and fix with its locating pin. Locate the chain over both cogs and weld the pedal bearing to the underside of the arm rest so that the chain is tight and in line. Weld a support bar between the wheel frame and the pedal bearing.

DIAGRAM 14

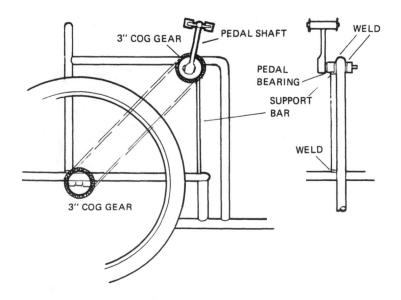

3'' COG GEAR   PEDAL SHAFT   WELD
PEDAL BEARING
SUPPORT BAR
WELD
3'' COG GEAR

BICYCLE AMBULANCE

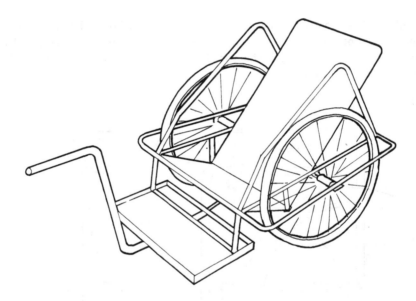

In conditions where motorised transport is rare or unpredictable this village-based ambulance can be useful in transporting a patient to a health centre or hospital within bicycle or animal power access (or of course to a place where other transport is available).

To the victim of an accident or burns, or to the women in obstructed labour, this might be the only sure means of reaching a health centre when the only alternative is the chance of a truck passing the village.

The towing bar can be designed appropriately for the means of pulling available (e.g. with a cross piece for towing by animal) and the carriage could have handles added at the rear if it is likely that it may be pushed on occasion.

Improvements would include a harness to hold the passenger firmly, padded seats and a reclining backrest with variable positions.

A simple method for attaching the tow bar of the ambulance to a bicycle.

Construction

Construct the wheel frame — Diagram 1; the arm rests — Diagram 2; and the foot rest support — Diagram 3.

    Materials: ¾'' conduit or ½'' GI tube.

DIAGRAM 1

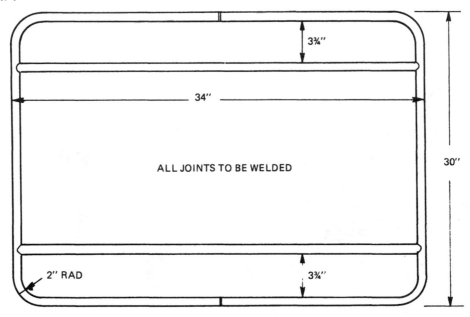

DIAGRAM 2

DIAGRAM 3

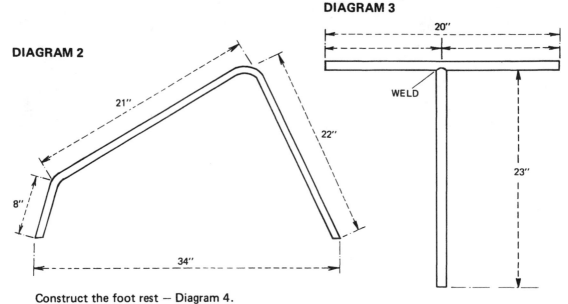

Construct the foot rest — Diagram 4.

    Materials: A — ¾'' conduit or ½'' GI tube
                    B — 1½'' X 1½'' X $^1/_8$'' mild steel angle.

DIAGRAM 4

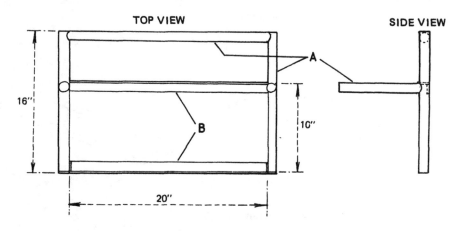

TOP VIEW   SIDE VIEW

16"   A   10"   B   20"

Construct the seat support — Diagram 5.

Materials: A — ¾" conduit or ½" GI tube
            B — 1½" X 1½" X $\frac{1}{8}$" mild steel angle.

DIAGRAM 5

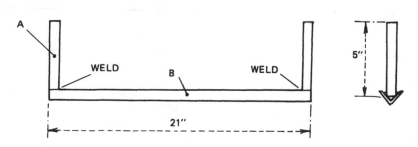

A   WELD   B   WELD   5"   21"

Construct the towing bar — Diagram 6.

Materials: 1" GI tube.

DIAGRAM 6

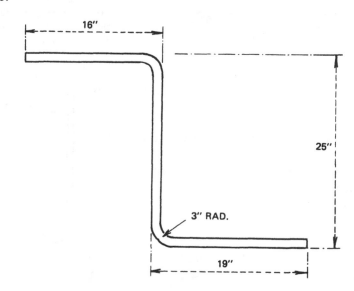

16"   25"   3" RAD.   19"

Cut out and weld wheel brackets to the wheel frame — Diagram 7.

Materials: 1½" X 1½" X ⅛" mild steel angle.

DIAGRAM 7

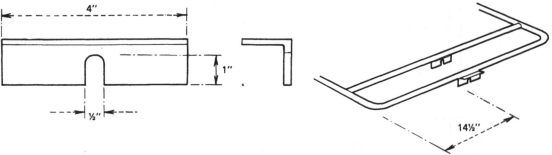

Cut out the seat, back and foot rests — Diagram 8.

Materials: ¼" plywood.

DIAGRAM 8

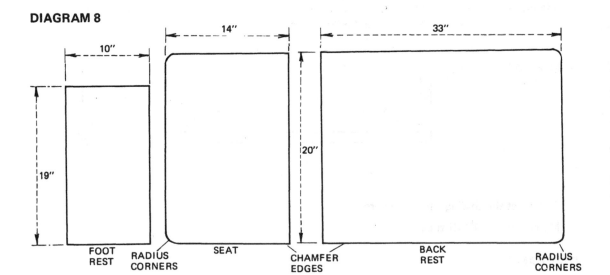

| FOOT REST | RADIUS CORNERS | SEAT | CHAMFER EDGES | BACK REST | RADIUS CORNERS |

DIAGRAM 9

Weld the arm rests to the wheel frame — Diagram 9.

Weld the foot rest and foot rest support to the wheel frame — Diagram 10.

DIAGRAM 10

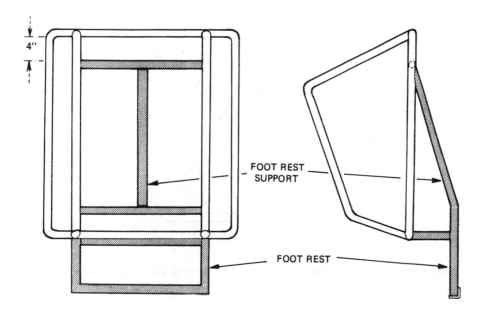

4"

FOOT REST
SUPPORT

FOOT REST

Weld the towing bar to the foot rest frame — Diagram 11.

DIAGRAM 11

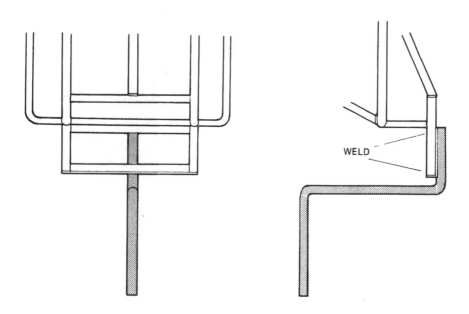

WELD

Weld a 20″ length of ¾″ conduit between arm rests as back rest support — Diagram 12.

DIAGRAM 12

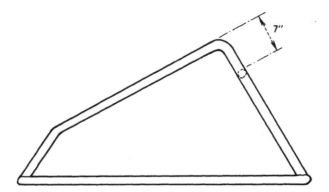

Attach the plywood seat, back and foot rests. Fix two standard 26″ bicycle wheels in their brackets. Clean welded areas and paint.

DRESSING/INSTRUMENT TROLLEY

A simple wheeled trolley will have many uses in the hospital wards and treatment areas including theatres.

Hooks or clips could be attached at either end to allow the easy fixing of large paper or plastic bags for disposal of dirty dressings etc.

The same basic design could be employed for many other uses. For example, the top tray could be replaced by a deep wooden box for use as an end-of-bed baby cot.

Construction

Make the components of the 'A' frame:

Diagram 1 — the two legs in ¾" conduit tube

Diagram 2 — the two struts in 1" X 1" mild steel square section

Diagram 3 — the two top pieces in 1" X 1" X ⅛" mild steel angle.

DIAGRAM 1

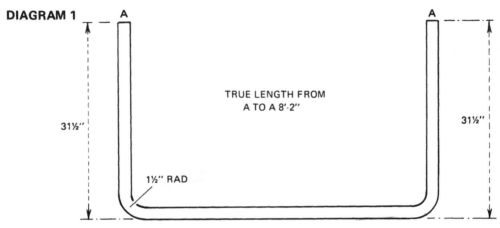

A

A

TRUE LENGTH FROM
A TO A 8'-2"

31½"

31½"

1½" RAD

DIAGRAM 2

2 HOLES DRILL ½" DIA
THRO' BOTH SIDES

1"

1"

18"

DIAGRAM 3

4"

RADIUS
ALL
CORNERS

Assemble the 'A' frame — Diagram 4.

DIAGRAM 4

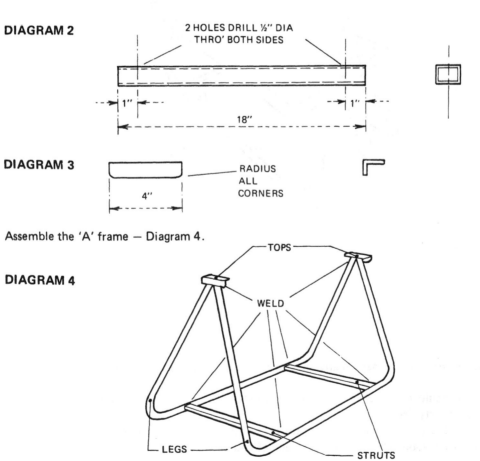

TOPS

WELD

LEGS

STRUTS

Construct the two tray frames — Diagram 5.

Materials: 1½″ X 1½″ X ⅛″ mild steel angle.

DIAGRAM 5

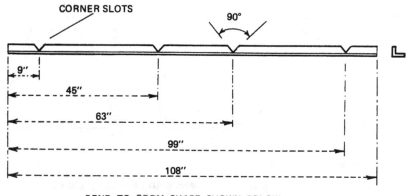

BEND TO FORM SHAPE SHOWN BELOW

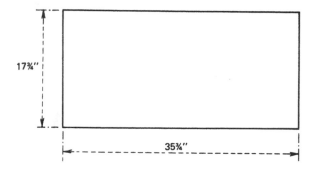

Make the tray platforms — Diagram 6.

Materials: ½″ plywood (with plastic finish if possible, otherwise well painted).

DIAGRAM 6

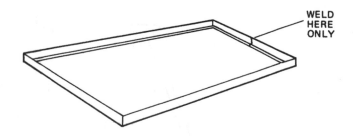

Weld the tray frame in position — Diagram 7.

DIAGRAM 7

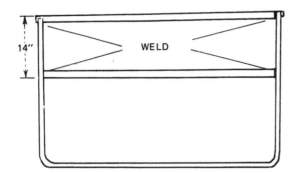
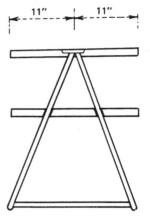

Attach the four wheels — Diagram 8.

Materials: Four 3″ diameter swivel type wheels with peg fitting and rubber rims.

Braze the wheels in position in the previously drilled holes in the frame struts ensuring free movement of the swivel.

DIAGRAM 8

Clean all welded areas and paint.

PATIENT'S TROLLEY

This functional patient's trolly incorporates adjustable side frames, variable stretcher inclination and removable drip stand for transfer to the patient's bed.

The stretcher tabletop is sheet steel but this could be replaced by a variety of other materials. Wheels can be of various sizes but should be rubber rimmed.

Construction

Construct the carriage frame — Diagram 1.

    Materials: ¾" GI tube.

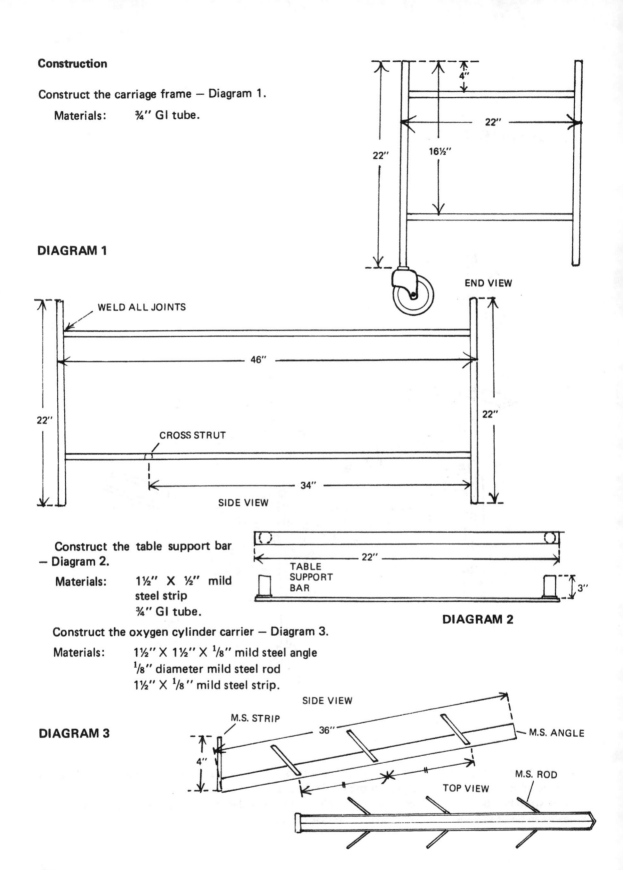

DIAGRAM 1

WELD ALL JOINTS

46"

22"

22"

CROSS STRUT

34"

SIDE VIEW

END VIEW

4"

22"

16½"

22"

Construct the table support bar — Diagram 2.

    Materials: 1½" X ½" mild steel strip
                  ¾" GI tube.

22"

TABLE SUPPORT BAR

3"

DIAGRAM 2

Construct the oxygen cylinder carrier — Diagram 3.

    Materials: 1½" X 1½" X ⅛" mild steel angle
                  ⅛" diameter mild steel rod
                  1½" X ⅛" mild steel strip.

SIDE VIEW

DIAGRAM 3

M.S. STRIP

36"

M.S. ANGLE

4"

M.S. ROD

TOP VIEW

Construct the two table stops — Diagram 4.

Materials: 2" X 2" angle.

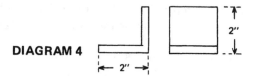

DIAGRAM 4

Construct the two transfusion scabbards — Diagram 5.

Materials: ¾" GI tube.

DIAGRAM 5

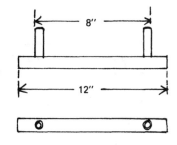

Attach these fittings to the carriage frame — Diagram 6.

DIAGRAM 6

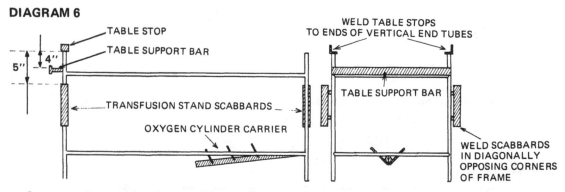

TABLE STOP
TABLE SUPPORT BAR
5"
4"
TRANSFUSION STAND SCABBARDS
OXYGEN CYLINDER CARRIER

WELD TABLE STOPS
TO ENDS OF VERTICAL END TUBES
TABLE SUPPORT BAR
WELD SCABBARDS
IN DIAGONALLY
OPPOSING CORNERS
OF FRAME

Construct the stretcher frame — Diagram 7.

Materials: ¾" GI tube
               ¾" conduit tube.

The two 19½" lengths must be assembled over the two 22" lengths of conduit before the latter are welded to the frame and should be free to rotate.

DIAGRAM 7

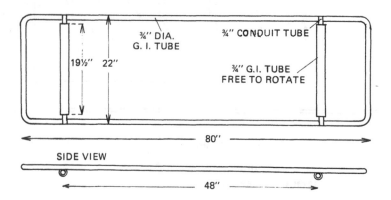

¾" DIA.
G. I. TUBE
¾" CONDUIT TUBE
19½"   22"
¾" G.I. TUBE
FREE TO ROTATE
80"
SIDE VIEW
48"

The stretcher top is made of 18 gauge GS plate bent around the stretcher frame and fixed on the underside with $\frac{1}{8}$" diameter pop rivets. The length of the stretcher top surface is 70" leaving 5" at each end.

Next construct the side bar holder — Diagram 8.

Materials: $\frac{3}{4}$" GI tube — A
2" X 1" mild steel section — B

DIAGRAM 8

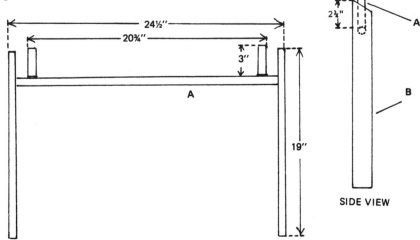

Construct the two side bars — Diagram 9.

Materials: $\frac{1}{8}$" diameter mild steel rod — A
$\frac{3}{4}$" conduit tube — B.

DIAGRAM 9

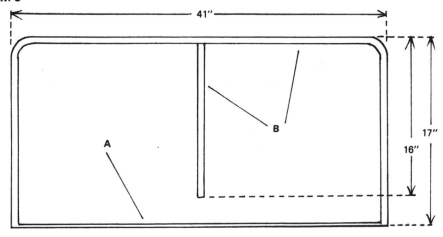

Construct the table height adjuster — Diagram 10.

Materials: 1$\frac{1}{2}$" X 1$\frac{1}{2}$" X $\frac{1}{8}$" mild steel angle — A
$\frac{1}{8}$" diameter mild steel rod — B.

DIAGRAM 10

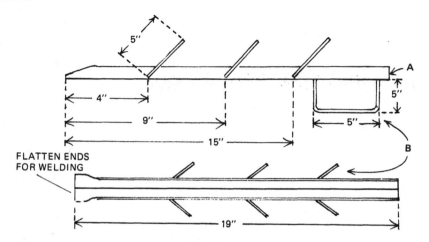

FLATTEN ENDS
FOR WELDING

Weld the table height adjuster to the centre of the front roller hinge on the stretcher table — Diagram 11. Weld the side bar holder to the main frame — but insert the centre vertical bar of the side bars into the holder before welding.

DIAGRAM 11

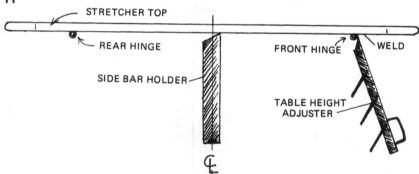

Locate the stretcher on the carriage frame and fix by welding at the rear roller hinge only i.e. the end away from the height adjuster.

Attach wheels, finish and paint.

BLOOD TRANSFUSION DRIP STAND

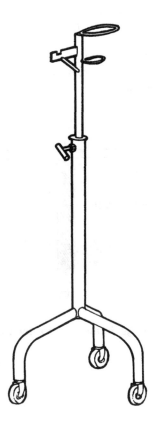

This free standing drip stand is adjustable for height. A simpler version could be made with a peg-and-hole arrangement to achieve varying height without the need to fit a locking screw.

An easier to weld arrangement could be designed for attaching the legs especially if wheels are not essential.

The top fittings can also be varied to suit different local containers.

Construction

Construct the main stand and attach fittings B and C as shown — Diagram 1.

Materials: 1″ galvanised iron tube — A
                    ³⁄₈″ Whitworth nut — B
                    Plain washer: 1½″ outside diameter, ¾″ inside diameter — C.

Drill a ³⁄₈″ diameter hole in one side only of the tube and weld B and C in position.

DIAGRAM 1

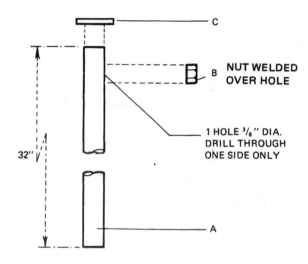

Make the locking screw — Diagram 2.

Materials: ³⁄₈″ mild steel rod — D
                    ³⁄₈″ Whitworth set pin (head removed) — E.

DIAGRAM 2

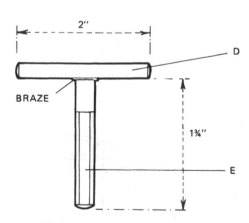

Construct the three main stand legs — Diagram 3
Materials: 1″ galvanised iron tube.

DIAGRAM 3

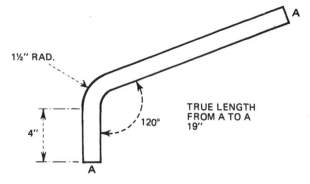

1½″ RAD.

4″

120°

A

A

TRUE LENGTH
FROM A TO A
19″

Construct the inner stand — Diagram 4.

Materials: ¾″ conduit tube.

DIAGRAM 4

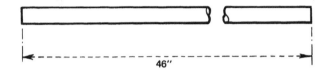

46″

Make the inner stand fittings — Diagram 5.

Materials: A, B and D — ¼″ diameter malleable iron rod
C — $^3/_{16}$″ X ¾″ mild steel strip.

DIAGRAM 5

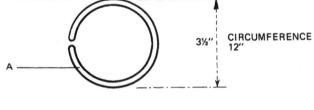

A

3½″

CIRCUMFERENCE
12″

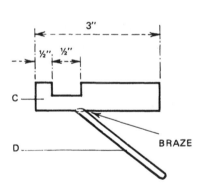

3″

½″ ½″

C

D

BRAZE

B

2″

CIRCUMFERENCE
7″

Assemble as shown — Diagram 6.

DIAGRAM 6

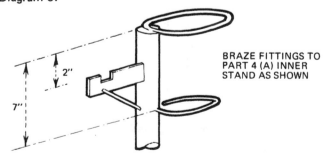

2″

7″

BRAZE FITTINGS TO
PART 4 (A) INNER
STAND AS SHOWN

Weld the main stand legs — Diagram 7.

DIAGRAM 7

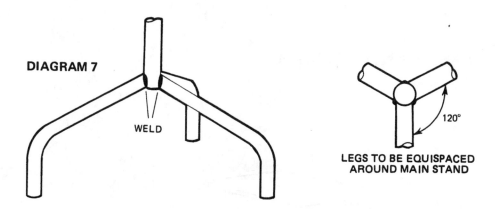

WELD

120°

LEGS TO BE EQUISPACED
AROUND MAIN STAND

Attach the wheels — Diagram 8.

Materials: Three 4″ wheels with swivel peg fittings and rubber tyres.

DIAGRAM 8

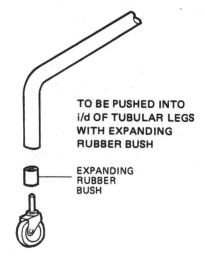

TO BE PUSHED INTO
i/d OF TUBULAR LEGS
WITH EXPANDING
RUBBER BUSH

EXPANDING
RUBBER
BUSH

Clean and paint.

BEDSIDE TABLE AND LOCKER

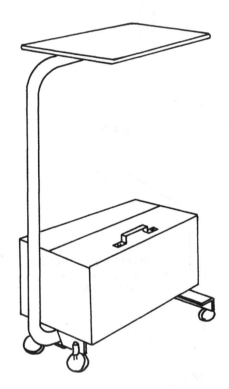

A movable bedside table and locker is a useful piece of basic equipment in all hospital wards.

Few design details are given here as the sizes should be matched to local needs and bed heights. It is quite possible to design a variable height table which can also be turned over the bed. This can be done for example with a locking screw arrangement similar to that shown in the previous design for a drip stand. However, this does introduce a good deal of stress and, in practice, has not proven very satisfactory. If the basic design can be sized so that the locker can fit under the bed (i.e. if it is not necessary to turn the table) this is preferable.

A good, strong alternative is to use an 'A' frame for the vertical support. Again, this cannot be adjusted for height.

Construction

The main frame should be 1½" galvanised iron tubing and the table and box supports should be 1½" X 1½" X ⅛" mild steel angle. The box and table top can be made from plywood and mild steel sheet. Care should be taken to allow the hinged lid to lie flat on the remainder of the box top when open to avoid strain on the hinges.

The main frame can be constructed as shown in Diagram 1, ensuring that the tubing is held exactly vertical for welding on the angle iron pieces. The box can be made in any number of ways depending on local needs and materials.

DIAGRAM 1

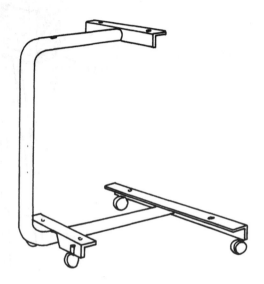

SUCTION PUMP

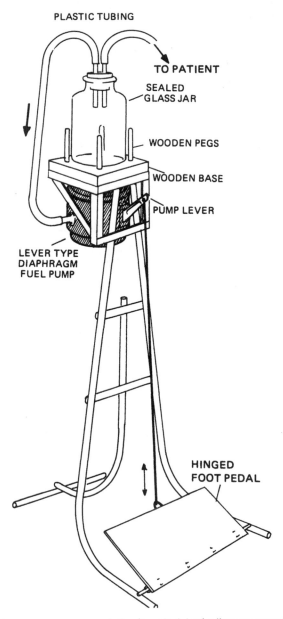

PLASTIC TUBING

TO PATIENT

SEALED
GLASS JAR

WOODEN PEGS

WOODEN BASE

PUMP LEVER

LEVER TYPE
DIAPHRAGM
FUEL PUMP

HINGED
FOOT PEDAL

A washable, mechanical suction pump will find many uses around the hospital including neonatal work and general use in operating theatres.

A simple pump can be designed around whatever kind of mechanical pump is available. This one shows a lever-type diaphragm pump such as is found on many cars and lorries. Since the pump itself is to pump air rather than the liquid it was made for, it is necessary to fill the chamber (the part not containing the valves !) with some hard setting material such as plaster.

The pump is suspended by an angle section framework attached to a square wooden block on which sits a glass jar. The pump is operated by a foot pedal connected by wire to the lever of the pump.

Plastic tubing is sealed into the airtight lid of the glass jar — old jam jars are suitable.

Such a pump is able to produce an easily controlled pressure differential of 15-25 cms Hg.

SUPINE EXERCISING MACHINE

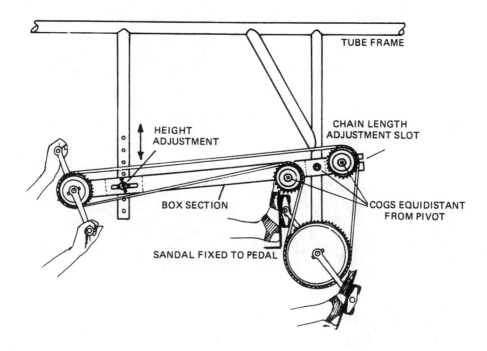

TUBE FRAME

HEIGHT
ADJUSTMENT

CHAIN LENGTH
ADJUSTMENT SLOT

BOX SECTION

COGS EQUIDISTANT
FROM PIVOT

SANDAL FIXED TO PEDAL

The mechanism of this exerciser is made from bicycle parts. It helps patients who are confined on their backs in beds to regain co-ordination between arm and leg movements and to exercise.

The height can be adjusted by means of a bolt (marked at A) slotted into holes in the overhead frame.

The mechanism is suspended from a large frame which can be wheeled into position over the patient's bed. Alternatively, it could be suspended from the ceiling and the patient's bed moved under it.

CALIPER

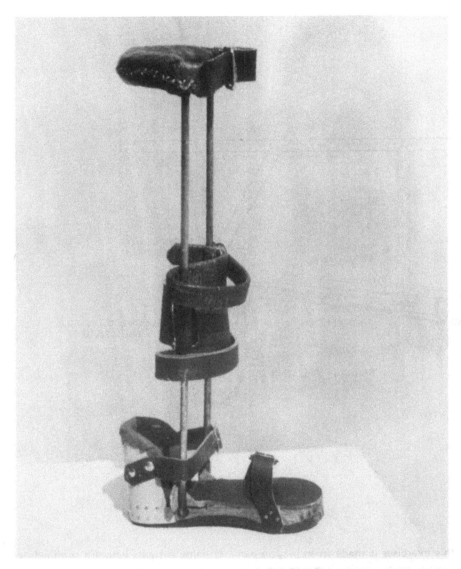

Calipers can be made from a variety of available materials. This photograph shows one made in quantity by the staff of the Instrument Engineering Department of the Ahmadu Bello University Teaching Hospital in Zaria, Nigeria. Materials include a wooden base, tyre sole, local leather inner sole and straps, steel concrete-reinforcing rod, plastic drainpipe heelpiece, etc.

The addition of the small metal stop shown in this example can be of help in the correction of footdrop — a condition often seen in very young mothers.

OTHER DESIGNS AND IDEAS *

*   Some of these designs were contributed by the Appropriate Health Resources & Technologies Action Group and the Disabilities Study Unit, and others appeared in the journal, *Appropriate Technology.*

INFANT WEIGHING SCALES

Simple scales such as those shown here can be of tremendous value in promoting positive maternal and child health. They can be used in conjunction with the 'road to health chart' approach and, indeed, could be calibrated in scales corresponding directly to these weight-for-age charts. (See Morley, D. *Paediatric Priorities in the Developing World,* Butterworths, 1973, 124 pp, or contact the Foundation for Teaching Aids at Low Cost).

Before beginning to build these scales, accurate standard weights must be prepared. Borrow some weights and a scale and make bags of dry sand or stones which weigh ¼ kilo (250 gms), ½ kilo (500 gms), 1 kilo, 2 kilos and 5 kilos. Two bags of each will be enough.

The baby holder is then made from a square of cotton, 750 mm wide, which is folded into a triangle and sewn (see Diagram 1). Buttonholes are made in each corner. Strong thin rope is tied to the right-angle corner and passed through the other two, and a loop is made at the free end for attaching to the scale.

A simply-made, robust infant weighing scale can be made from a metre of hardwood, about 20 mm square, and three bent (and blunted) nails — Diagram 1.

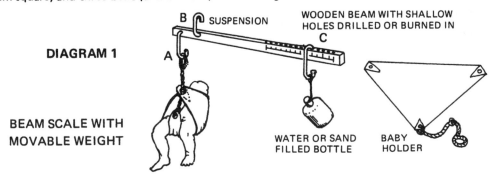

DIAGRAM 1

BEAM SCALE WITH
MOVABLE WEIGHT

B   SUSPENSION

WOODEN BEAM WITH SHALLOW
HOLES DRILLED OR BURNED IN

C

A

WATER OR SAND
FILLED BOTTLE

BABY
HOLDER

The principle of the beam scale is that a large weight (the baby) a small distance from the point of suspension (the fulcrum) is counter-balanced by a small weight suspended a greater distance from the fulcrum.

Two holes are drilled through the beam about 25 mm and 75 mm from one end. Strong hooks made from 150 mm blunted nails are passed through the holes and serve as the fulcrum (B) and the point of attachment of the child holder (A). The size of the hook is not important, but it must pivot freely in the hole. The scale is then ready for calibrating.

The movable counter-balance is then made from a bottle filled to a graduation mark with water or sand. The crucial point is that it needs to weigh about 1 kg. With the beam suspended from hook B and a standard 1 kg. weight attached to hook A, the counter-balance (C) is attached to the beam and moved until the beam is horizontal and in equilibrium. A pencil mark is made at this point.

Additional weights are then added sequentially to (A) and the process repeated. Alternatively, after finding the 1 kg graduation mark, the 1 kg. weight attached to (A) is replaced by 15 kgs and the 15 kg. graduation mark determined. The distance between these two marks is then divided into 14 equal lengths. The scale will then be graduated in 1 kg. divisions as far as 15 kgs. Finally, drill or burn holes at each mark, deep and wide enough for the weight hook to slip in and be secure.

A slightly more sophisticated weighing scale employing the same principle is shown in Diagram 2. It is more compact and the weight can be read directly. The scale is made from a quarter circle of plywood, reinforced with sheet metal at the corner where the pivot holes are drilled. The pivot holes (A) and (B) are about 20 mm apart. The weight is an iron bar weighing between 1 and 2 kgs. The instrument can be made less cumbersome by omitting the weight arm if a suitable heavy weight can be attached directly to the top corner of the top corner of the disc, i.e. where Diagram 2 shows the thumbscrews. The scale is calibrated by adding weights sequentially to the child holder and marking the scale in pencil initially and more permanently later.

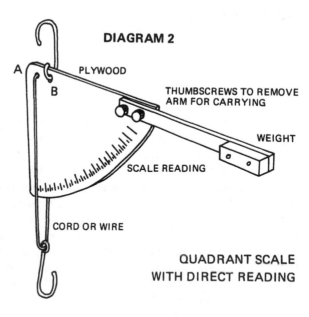

DIAGRAM 2

PLYWOOD

THUMBSCREWS TO REMOVE ARM FOR CARRYING

WEIGHT

SCALE READING

CORD OR WIRE

QUADRANT SCALE WITH DIRECT READING

If reliable springs can be obtained cheaply, a very easily carried scale can be made as shown in Diagram 3. The ideal spring would start about 300 mm long and compress to half that length under a load of 15 kgs. The spring is housed loosely in a piece of thick strong bamboo. To guard against the danger of splitting, the bamboo could be bound at each end. Because the spring is likely to be affected by the elements and to become inaccurate over a period of time, the scale should be checked at frequent intervals against standard weights. If it is discovered that it has become inaccurate, the scale may be recalibrated or the spring re-utilised in another casing.

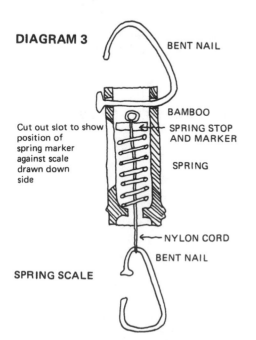

DIAGRAM 3

BENT NAIL

BAMBOO

SPRING STOP AND MARKER

Cut out slot to show position of spring marker against scale drawn down side

SPRING

NYLON CORD

BENT NAIL

SPRING SCALE

Designed by Jack Procter
for the Appropriate Health Resources and
Technologies Action Group,
85 Marylebone High Street,
London W1M 3DE.

SAND BED

A simple sand bed can be of great assistance for a number of conditions requiring longer-term nursing and in which the patient benefits from a redistribution of weight over the maximum body area to avoid pressure points.

These conditions include, for example, states of immobility such as spinal or multiple injury, serious arthritis, senility, etc., as well as states requiring the absorption of body fluids such as established decubitus ulcers (bed sores), superficial burns or incontinence. Sand bed nursing has achieved great success in the prevention of bed sores even in cases where the risk of decubitus ulceration is considered to be high. Soiled sand can easily be removed and replaced.

A sand bed is simply a bed-sized wooden tray containing sand and covered with a loose bed sheet. It can be supported on a conventional bed frame or on any sturdy tressle arrangement to achieve the required height. The sand should be of the softest possible quality with, ideally, an average particle size of a little less than 0.5 mm. The depth of the sand should be about 5 in (12 cm) and the depth of the tray an inch or two more to prevent spillage.

Reference:
I.M. Stewart,
Consultant Orthopaedic Surgeon,
Law Hospital,
Carluke, Lanarkshire,
Scotland.

A more detailed discussion of the sand bed can be found in Stewart, I.M., Sand Bed Nursing, *Tropical Doctor,* 7,69-72,1977.

LOW PRESSURE AIR BED

This air bed aims to solve similar nursing problems to the sand bed. In this case, the air bed maintains a constant pressure despite changes in the patient's posture and in the surface area of the body in contact with the bed.

Whilst a number of sophisticated and expensive air beds are available from commercial firms, this design achieves much the same result using simpler components.

Two standard, and readily available, camping air-mattresses of the box-edge type are placed one above the other on a wooden base. Two are required for the average patient to prevent 'bottoming' when they run at low pressure. The two air mattresses are connected together by tubing which in turn is connected to a standard aquarium aeration pump. A further length of tubing is connected to the air line by means of a 'T' piece. This joins a small metal tube bent into a circular shape in which have been drilled a number of small holes. This is immersed to a given depth in a column of water (see Diagram 1). Within about fifteen or twenty minutes after switching on the pump both mattresses become fully inflated and the pressure inside them is regulated by the depth to which the side tube is immersed in the column of liquid. If a person is now placed on the mattress the consequent rise in pressure will force air to bubble out of the system from the end of the tube until the pressure is once more at the pre-set level. Any further change in posture will result in more excess air bubbling out, or else a pause in the discharge from the tube until the pressure has built up once more to the required pressure. In the steady state condition the air from the pump bubbles out from the tube, and the pump then acts in the way it is designed to do in the aquarium.

DIAGRAM 1

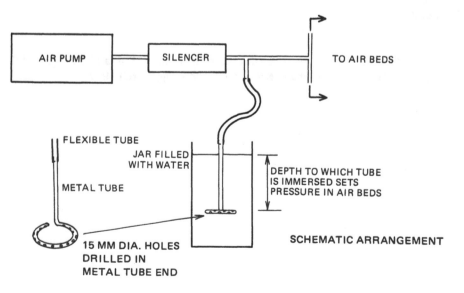

AIR PUMP

SILENCER

TO AIR BEDS

FLEXIBLE TUBE

JAR FILLED WITH WATER

METAL TUBE

DEPTH TO WHICH TUBE IS IMMERSED SETS PRESSURE IN AIR BEDS

15 MM DIA. HOLES DRILLED IN METAL TUBE END

SCHEMATIC ARRANGEMENT

In use it has been found possible and safe for patients who would normally be turned every two hours to be allowed to sleep through the night without being turned at all; the benefit to the patient and family of a complete night's sleep, or the benefit of a reduction of the load on the nursing staff, is considerable.

The technology is so obvious and simple that no worry is imposed on the users by the system; the pump is designed for continuous use and the only precaution required is a weekly check on the level of the water.

DIAGRAM 2

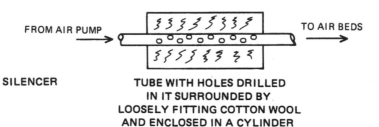

FROM AIR PUMP →   TO AIR BEDS →

SILENCER   TUBE WITH HOLES DRILLED
IN IT SURROUNDED BY
LOOSELY FITTING COTTON WOOL
AND ENCLOSED IN A CYLINDER

A further advantage of the system is that if it is necessary to carry out nursing procedures with the patient on the bed, further depression of the exhaust tube in the column of water for five minutes or so, or closing off the discharge line, is adequate to change the soft bed into a stiff surface. Experience has shown that immersion of the end of the tube to a depth of 75 mm to 100 mm is satisfactory for normal use.

Refinements to this basic design include the use of plastic foam surrounding the mattress to achieve more lateral stability. Also a small silencer can be made as shown above to reduce the vibration transmitted to the bed.

Reference:
K. J. McCubbin and D. C. Simpson,
Orthopaedic Bio-Engineering Unit,
Princess Margaret Rose Orthopaedic Hospital,
Fairmilehead,
Edinburgh EH1O 7EP.

A more detailed discussion can be found in: McCubbin, K.J. and Simpson, D.C., A Low Pressure Air Bed, *Journal of Medical Engineering and Technology*, March 1977.

PHOTOTHERAPY BOX FOR NEONATAL JAUNDICE

Neonatal jaundice is a common problem in various parts of Africa and elsewhere where it is often associated with low birth weight. Whilst phototherapy cannot replace the exchange blood transfusion required for severly jaundiced neonates, the facilities for such transfusions are restricted to a few centres. In local rural hospitals or in maternity posts phototherapy can be used both to reduce the number of jaundiced babies it is necessary to refer to such centres and to reduce the severity of the symptoms in such children.

A simple phototherapy box can be made from wood as shown in the diagram or from available local materials. It consists essentially of an inverted tray containing six 40 Watt daylight fluorescent tubes. The precise dimensions of the design can be varied to suit local needs, but in general the light tray (A in the sketch) should be suspended approximately 18" above the baby in the cot or incubator. Use of this box by unskilled personnel requires proper instruction and, in particular, the infant's eyes must be covered at all times.

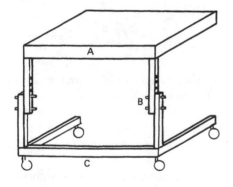

A. Inverted wooden box, 140 cm X 75 cm X 20 cm containing six 40 Watt daylight fluorescent tubes mounted parallel to the longest side.
The box is lined with a white reflecting surface so that the light is directed downwards.
B. Adjustable wooden supports fixed by strong pegs to vary the heights of A so that the unit can be used over cots or incubators.
C. Base fitted with wheels for easy mobility.

Reference:
Jenny Mee, Department of Paediatrics, Ahmadu Bello University Hospital, Zaria, Nigeria.
David Scott, Wesley Guild Hospital, Ilesha, Nigeria.

A more detailed account can be found in: Mee, J. and Scott, D., Phototherapy for Neonatal Jaundice in Rural Africa, *Tropical Doctor,* 7, 33-34, 1977.

THERMOPLASTIC AIDS

Short lengths of plastic drainpipe can be used as the material for a number of medical and rehabilitation aids.

The Port Harcourt Christian Council Project has made a variety of successful aids including splints, cervical collars, spinal jackets, etc.

With experiment, standard templates can be developed made of heavy paper or light card. These are used to mark an appropriate-sized piece of plastic pipe with a felt-tipped pen.

CHILD'S SPINAL JACKET

FOREARM SPLINT

CERVICAL COLLAR

A hand-held hack-saw blade, used so that it cuts when being pulled, is a fairly easy means of completing the roughing-out stage. Filing and scraping with a sharpened hack-saw blade will give a smooth rounded edge. The material is in the shape of a section of pipe at this stage. Using heat-resisting gloves the material is hand-worked over a gas ring. The process is actually a simple type of stretch-forming. A few smoothed wooden anvil shapes will help but once the temperature is just right the manual strength needed is quite small.

Three ways of heating the plastic can be tried. A boiling water bath provides exactly the right temperature but has the disadvantage of not localising the heat. A bench-mounted welding torch on a low flame provides very good localision of heat but easily burns the plastic. A bottle-gas ring is a fair compromise and there is very little trouble with burning. This latter method is the one recommended.

Plastic is in many ways an ideal material for such aids. It is waterproof, strong, cheap, reusable and adjustable. If stock sizes are made the nurse or health worker can select an appropriate size and, by gently heating, can adjust it for a perfect fitting for the individual patient. After use, the aid can be taken back into stock. A particularly useful role for this method is in providing children with spinal support jackets. Compared with the hot and heavy alternative of plaster that goes soggy during the rain season, plastic has much to offer. For this use, the plastic corset should be drilled for lacing and ventilation and worn over a T-shirt or vest.

Reference:
Davies, M., IT Surburban Style in Africa, *Appropriate Technology,* Vol. 3, No. 1.

BABY INCUBATOR

This baby incubator is the result of a search for a cheap, simple, safe device for nursing premature and sick babies. In areas of many developing countries air temperature and humidity are low, conditions which may be fatal to small babies. In addition the risks of infection are lowered if an incubator is properly used.

Five of the incubators described here have been in use at Mvumi Hospital in Tanzania for over three years and have proved satisfactory.

The central feature of the incubator is a group of four standard electric light bulbs which control temperature, humidity, and circulation of the air.

1. *Temperature* Two bulbs are each 40 watts and are alight constantly. The other two are each 100 watts and switched on and off by a thermostat. (In our models a Gallenkamp Compenstat type TM 500.)

   In this way up to three bulbs can burn out and there will still be at least 40 watts of heat — sufficient to maintain an adequate temperature for a short period.

2. *Humidity* is provided by a tray containing water, mounted over the light bulbs and heated by them. It is designed to minimise the risk of spilling over the bulbs and can be filled while the incubator is operating, by lifting a cover at the front.

3. *Circulation* of air is by simple convection. Air enters through an insect-wire screen beneath the light bulbs, rises as it is warmed and escapes through screened holes in the top of the canopy. No circulating fan is necessary.

Points in Construction. The canopy is made of ¼" Perspex which can be cut with a fine saw and bent to shape as follows:

The Perspex is placed on a wooden bench with the edge of the bench under the line along which the Perspex is to be bent, and a weight (e.g. bricks) holding it down on the bench. It is then slowly heated by moving a gas burner back and forth along the line until it softens and can be bent to 90°. It must be held in this position until it cools, e.g by packing a weight against it. The ends of the canopy are cut to shape and can be attached with a glue made by dissolving pieces of Perspex in enough chloroform or acetone to make a very thick solution — best applied with an old hypodermic syringe. Corner brackets of aluminium or brass are necessary. The best hinges for the canopy and its doors are brass piano hinges, but any available type will do.

The light bulb sockets are preferably of the brass and ceramic type as plastic ones do not stand the heat well.

Thin gauge aluminium is best for the inner and outer linings of the heating box, and for the

(Continued on page 83)

DIAGRAM 1: FRONT VIEW WITHOUT CANOPY

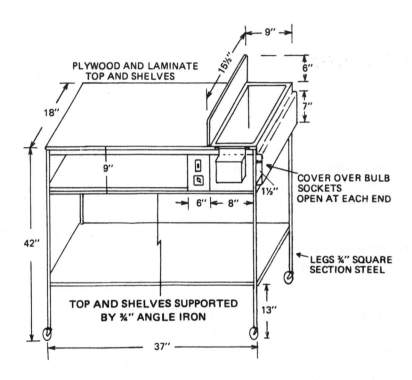

PLYWOOD AND LAMINATE
TOP AND SHELVES

9″

15½″

6″

7″

18″

9″

COVER OVER BULB
SOCKETS
OPEN AT EACH END

1½″

42″

6″ 8″

LEGS ¾″ SQUARE
SECTION STEEL

TOP AND SHELVES SUPPORTED
BY ¾″ ANGLE IRON

13″

37″

DIAGRAM 2: PERSPEX CANOPY

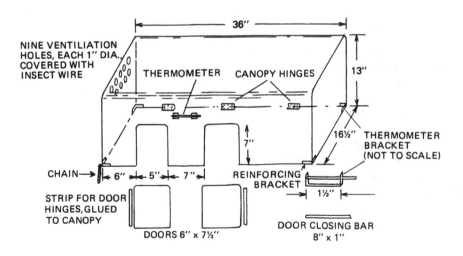

NINE VENTILIATION
HOLES, EACH 1″ DIA.,
COVERED WITH
INSECT WIRE

THERMOMETER   CANOPY HINGES

36″

13″

7″

16½″   THERMOMETER
BRACKET
(NOT TO SCALE)

CHAIN   6″   5″   7″

REINFORCING
BRACKET

STRIP FOR DOOR
HINGES, GLUED
TO CANOPY

1½″

DOORS 6″ x 7½″

DOOR CLOSING BAR
8″ x 1″

DIAGRAM 3: HUMIDIFIER COVER

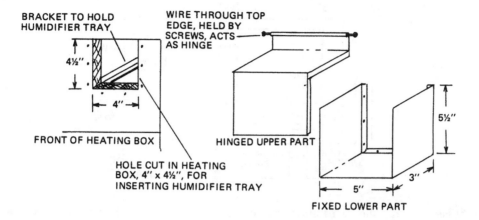

BRACKET TO HOLD HUMIDIFIER TRAY

WIRE THROUGH TOP EDGE, HELD BY SCREWS, ACTS AS HINGE

4½"

4"

FRONT OF HEATING BOX

HOLE CUT IN HEATING BOX, 4" x 4½", FOR INSERTING HUMIDIFIER TRAY

HINGED UPPER PART

5½"

3"

5"

FIXED LOWER PART

frame angle iron and square section steel rod is ideal. (The original models had the horizontal surfaces made of plywood covered with white laminate.)

The whole construction can be simplified and made cheaper if painted wood is used and the canopy can be of heavy clear plastic sheeting on a wooden frame.

The humidifier tray is most easily made from a sheet of light gauge aluminium or copper bent to shape over a block of wood the exact size of the tray. A better method is to use heavier gauge copper or brass, soldered or brazed. A spare tray is advisable so one can be boiled and cleaned each day to maintain sterility.

The baby tray is made of a sheet of plywood or hardwood, 14" X 24" with a wooden edging 1" high by ½" wide. The baby lies on a 1" thick foam mattress covered with plastic sheeting. Hooks on the tray fit into loops on the partition so that one end of the tray can be elevated as necessary.

In the original models the thermostat bulb was situated over the partition so that the temperature of the incoming air activated the thermostat switch. This was found to give stable temperatures.

Operation The incubator is switched on and allowed to stabilise for about half an hour, then the thermostat dial is set to the temperature shown by the thermometer. Then it is set to the required operating temperature, usually 36°.

DIAGRAM 4: HUMIDIFIER TRAY (LEFT)
DETAIL OF PARTITION (RIGHT)

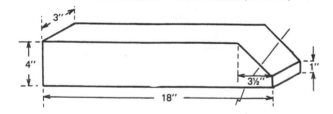

3"

4"

3½"

1"

18"

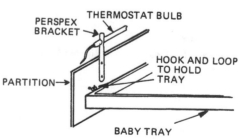

PERSPEX BRACKET

THERMOSTAT BULB

HOOK AND LOOP TO HOLD TRAY

PARTITION →

BABY TRAY

DIAGRAM 5: WIRING DIAGRAM

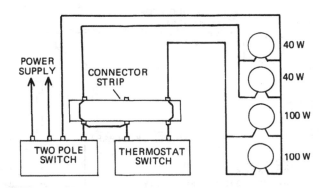

The humidifier tray should be emptied, cleaned and preferably boiled at least once per week, preferably daily. Only soft, clean water or rain water should be used in the humidifier. A depth of about one inch is adequate and the level should be checked, along with the light bulbs and temperature, at regular intervals. This is most easily done by making these three items part of the regular infant care routine, along with feeding, turning, observations, etc.

Burnt out light bulbs should be replaced as soon as possible. The incubator should be switched off while this is being done. Access to bulbs is by undoing the insect screen underneath.

DIAGRAM 6: CROSS-SECTION OF HEATING/HUMIDIFYING BOX

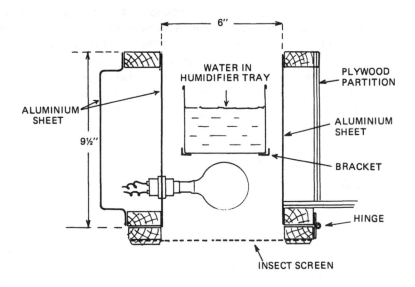

Reference:
Bolliger, P., Design for a Simple Baby Incubator, *Appropriate Technology,* Vol 4, No. 2, August 1977.

CHAIR WITH WHEELS

This chair and the walking frame on the following page are two examples of equipment designed for use by physically handicapped children in Jahore, West Malaysia. Both are made from locally available rattan and bamboo but could easily be adapted for construction in other materials.

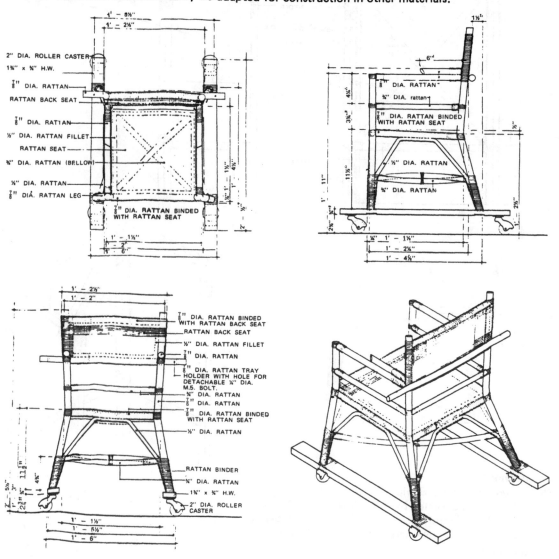

WALKING FRAME

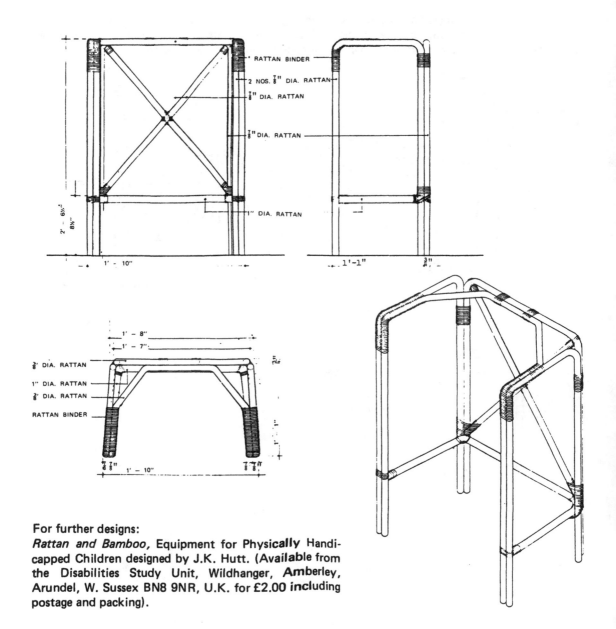

For further designs:
Rattan and Bamboo, Equipment for Physically Handicapped Children designed by J.K. Hutt. (Available from the Disabilities Study Unit, Wildhanger, Amberley, Arundel, W. Sussex BN8 9NR, U.K. for £2.00 including postage and packing).

Printed in the USA
CPSIA information can be obtained
at www.ICGtesting.com
JSHW052019140824
68134JS00027B/2555